Crochet Flower Garden

Creative Patterns for Floral Masterpieces

CONTENTS

INTRODUCTION 1

SUPPLIES 2

STITCHES 6

ABBREVIATIONS 16

PATTERNS... 17

SUNFLOWER 18

AGROSTEMMA GITHAGO
25

PRINCESS SUKI ROSE
30

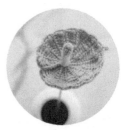

PINK CHAMPION
36

BIG THAI ROSE
41

NARCISSUS
49

DANDELION
54

AISHA ROSE
59

GESANG
64

DAHLIA
68

INTRODUCTION

Welcome to "Crochet Flower Garden: Creative Patterns for Floral Masterpieces," where the beauty of nature meets the art of crochet. This book is a celebration of floral designs, offering you a delightful collection of patterns that range from simple, elegant blooms to intricate, breathtaking masterpieces. Whether you're a seasoned crocheter or just starting your journey, this book provides the perfect blend of creativity and technique to help you craft stunning floral creations.

"Crochet Flower Garden: Creative Patterns for Floral Masterpieces" is more than just a pattern book; it's an invitation to explore the artistic side of crochet. As you flip through these pages, you'll not only develop new skills but also find joy in the meditative process of creating something beautiful with your hands.

So, grab your hook and yarn, and step into the world of crochet flowers. Whether you're making them for yourself, for loved ones, or simply for the joy of creating, this book will guide you through the wonderful journey of bringing a crochet flower garden to life. Happy crocheting!

SUPPLIES

YARN

When it comes to crochet, there are many different types of yarn to choose from. You can find it in a huge variety of textures, colors, weights, and fiber content.

Texture: If you're a beginner, it's smart to choose with yarns that are easy to work with: nothing too fluffy, fine, silky, slippery, or bumpy! You can practice with more textured or delicate fibers as your crochet skills advance.

Color: Yarn is available in a rainbow of colors, including solids, self-striping, and multicolor yarn. Beginners should start with yarns in a lighter color, so it's easier to see your stitches!

Weight: There are seven yarn weight categories: Lace (0), superfine (1), fine (2), DK/light (3), medium (4 – also known as worsted weight), bulky (5), super bulky (6), and jumbo (7).

STITCH MARKERS

Stitch markers are small tools that you'll use to mark your stitches as you crochet. You can use stitch markers to mark the beginning of a round, the end of a row, or to keep track of increases and decreases.

NEEDLE

Crocheting is done with a single hook (unlike knitting, which requires two needles).

When it comes to shopping for the best crochet hooks, you have a lot of options. Crochet hooks come in a variety of materials, shapes, and sizes – each with its own pros and cons.

If you're on a budget, you can even make your own stitch markers out of paper clips or bobby pins.

HOT MELT ADHESIVE

Mechanical hot-melt glue guns are the ideal tools for producing flower arrangements, wreaths, garlands and decorations

FLOWER STEM

The stem is created by wrapping floristry wire with tape. The petals are sewn together and then the stem is inserted into the middle and sewn around.

IRON WIRE

Either floral wire or stainless steel is going to be your best bet. Copper is cheap and easiest to bend, but it can and will tarnish and turn your yarn green. Same with brass or most nickel alloys. Floral wire is going to have a coating that prevents tarnish, but might not be stiff enough to provide the structure you need. Stainless steel (aircraft wire/lock wire) does not tarnish, and comes in many weights so you can choose which you need.

NEEDLE

A yarn needle is a large, blunt-tipped needle that you'll use to weave in the ends of your yarn and sew pieces of crochet together. A yarn needle may also be called a darning needle or a tapestry needle.

COTTON STUFFING

It gives a great shape, without bumps on the surface of your stuffed crochet. You can use other stuffing like old pillow stuffing, yarn scraps etc.

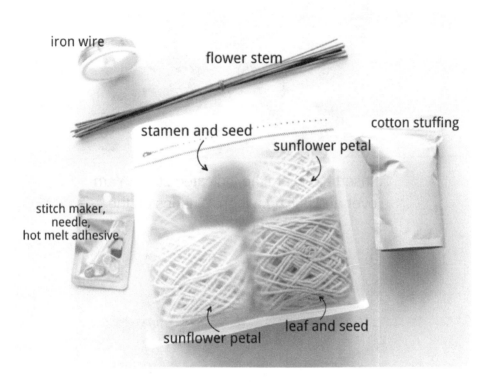

iron wire

flower stem

stamen and seed

sunflower petal

cotton stuffing

stitch maker,
needle,
hot melt adhesive

sunflower petal

leaf and seed

STARTER KITS

STITCHES

SINGLE DECREASE (SC2TOG)

1. Insert hook into the indicated stitch. Yarn over and pull up a loop. (2 loops on the hook.)

2. Insert hook into the next stitch. Yarn over and pull up a loop. (3 loops on the hook.) Yarn over, pull through all 3 loops on the hook.

TREBLE (TR)

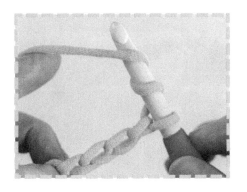

1. Yarn over the hook twice (this means wrapping the yarn around the hook from back to front two times). Your hook should now have three loops on it.

2. Then, skip four chains and insert the hook into the fifth chain from the hook. (The four skipped chains count as the first stitch.)

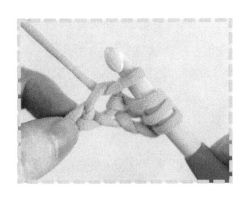

3. Then, yarn over again and pull up a loop. You should now have four loops on your hook.

4. Yarn over again and pull through two loops. You should now have three loops remaining on your hook.

TREBLE (TR)

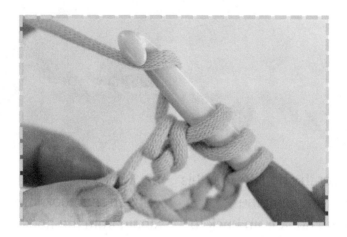

5. Yarn over again and pull through two loops. You should now have two loops remaining on your hook.

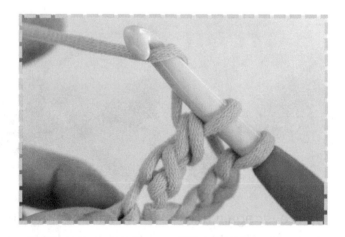

6. Finally, yarn over one last time and pull through the remaining two loops. Congratulations, you've just made your first treble crochet stitch!

HALF DOUBLE CROCHET STITCH (HDC)

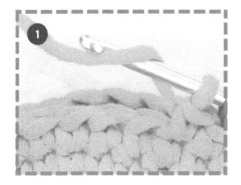

1. Yarn over

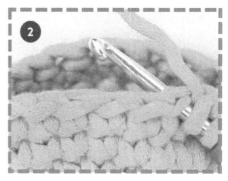

2. Insert the hook under top loops of the next stitch.

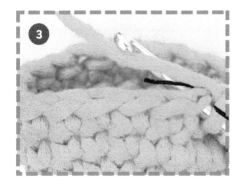

3. Yarn over. Pull the yarn through the stitch to draw up a loop.

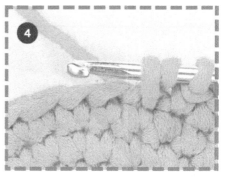

4. There should be three loops on the hook.

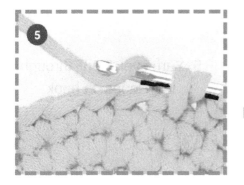

5. Yarn over. Pull the yarn through all three loops on the hook. There should be one loop left on the hook.

BACK LOOP SINGLE (BLO SC)

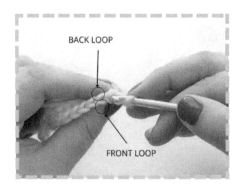

1. Identify the front & the back loop

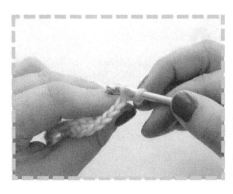

2. Insert hook in back loop

3. Yarn over

4. Pull up a loop

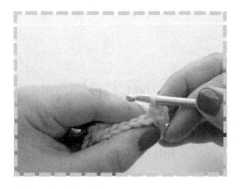

5. Yarn over & pull through both loops on hook

BACK LOOP HALF DOUBLE (BLO HDC)

1. Yarn over from back to front to start the BLhdc

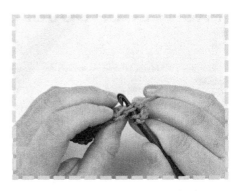

2. Identify the front and back loop

3. Insert crochet hook through the back loop only

4. Pull up a loop

5. Yarn Over

6. Pull hook through all 3 loops – BLhdc is finished

FRONT LOOP DOUBLE (FLO DC)

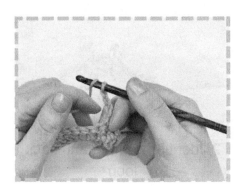

1. Yarn over from back to front

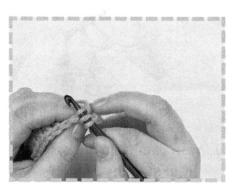

3. Insert the crochet hook into the front loop only

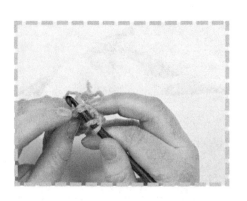

2. Identify the front loop

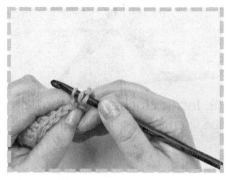

4. Pull up a loop

FRONT LOOP DOUBLE (FLO DC)

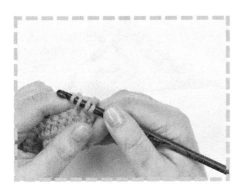

5. Yarn over

7. Yarn over

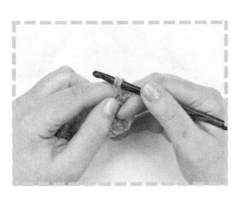

6. Pull yarn through the first 2 loops on the crochet hook

8. Pull yarn through the last 2 loops on the crochet hook

BACK LOOP DOUBLE (BLO DC)

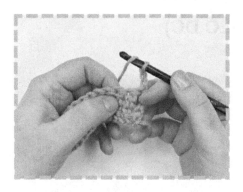

1. Yarn over from back to front

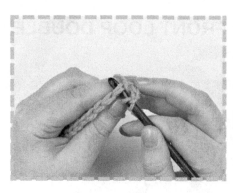

2. Identify the back loop

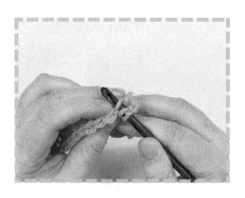

3. Insert the crochet hook into
the back loop only

4. Pull up a loop

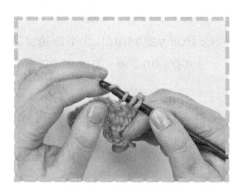

5. Yarn over

BACK LOOP DOUBLE (BLO DC)

6. Pull yarn through the first 2 loops on the crochet hook

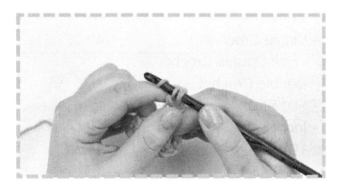

7. Yarn over

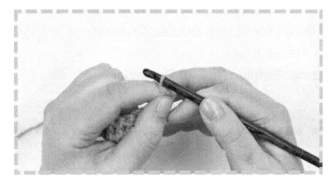

8. Pull yarn through the last 2 loops on the crochet hook

ABBREVIATIONS

Crochet pattern is written using U.S. crochet terminology.

- ch – Chain
- sc – Single Crochet
- hdc – Half Double Crochet
- dc – Double Crochet
- ss – Slip Stitch
- inc - Increase
- dec – Decrease
- blo sc – Back Loop Single Crochet
- blo hdc – Back Loop Half Double Crochet
- blo dc – Back Loop Double Crochet
- flo dc – Front Loop Double Crochet
- tr – Treble Stitch
- sc2tog: Single Crochet Decrease

PATTERNS

SUNFLOWER

Materials

- Yarn – yarn of 3 color, pink, khaki and green
- Hook – 2 mm or 2.5 mm
- Flower Rod – 16 inches long x 0.08 inches diameter (40cm x 2mm)
- Scissors

- Iron wire – 6 inches long x 0.02 inches diameter (15cm x 0.4mm)
- Stitch marker
- Darning needle
- Hot melt adhesive

STAMEN

Start with a magic ring
R1: work 6 sc into the magic ring, 1 ss, 1 ch. [6]
R2: *2 sc in each st*, after the first set, then repeat ** 5 times, 1 ss, 1 ch. [12]
R3: *1 sc, 2 sc in each st*, after the first set, then repeat ** 5 times, 1 ss, 1 ch. [18]
R4: *1 sc, 2 sc in each st, 1 sc*, after the first set, then repeat ** 5 times, 1 ss, 1 ch. [24]
R5: *3 sc, 2 sc in each st*, after the first set, then repeat ** 5 times, 1 ss, 1 ch. [30]

R6: Place a stitch marker and keep it here *blo sc 2, blo sc 2 in each st, blo sc 2*, after the first set, then repeat * * 5 times, 1 ss, 1 ch. [36]
R7: *blo sc 5, blo sc 2 in each st* , after the first set, then repeat ** 5 times, 1 ss, 1 ch. [42]
R8: *blo sc 3, blo sc 2 in each st, blo sc 3*, after the first set, then repeat **5 times, 1 ss, 1 ch. [48]
R9: * blo sc 7, blo sc 2 in each st*, after the first set, then repeat ** 5 times, 1 ss, 1 ch. [54]
R10: blo sc 54, 1 ss, 1 ch, cut and leave a tail. [54]

MELON SEED

Go back to R6, where you placed an st marker. working in front loops of stamen only
R6: *ch 3, 1 ss at the base of the ch, sk 1, 1 ss into the next st* repeat ** till end of row, 1 ss in next row
R7 – R9: Repeat R6 (Place a stitch marker and keep it here), 1 ss, 1 ch, cut and leave a tail

FLOWER SEPAL

Start with a magic ring
R1: work 6 sc into the magic ring, 1 ss, 1 ch. [6]
R2 – R3: 6 sc, 1 ss, 1 ch. [6]
R4: *2 sc in each st*, after the first set, then repeat ** 5 times, 1 ss, 1 ch. [12]
R5: *1 sc, 2 sc in each st*, after the first set, then repeat ** 5 times, 1 ss, 1 ch. [18]
R6: *1 sc, 2 sc in each st, sc*, after the first set, then repeat ** 5 times, 1 ss, 1 ch. [24]
R7: *sc 3, 2 sc in each st*, after the first set, then repeat ** 5 times, 1 ss, 1 ch. [30]
R8: *sc 2, 2 sc in each st, sc2*, after the first set, then repeat **5 times, 1 ss, 1 ch. [36]
R9: *sc 5, 2 sc in each st*, after the first set, then repeat ** 5 times, 1 ss, 1 ch. [42]
R10: *sc 3, 2 sc in each st, sc 3*, after the first set, then repeat ** 5 times, 1 ss, 1 ch. [48]
R11: *sc 7, 2 sc in each st*; after the first set, then repeat ** 5 times, 1 ss, 1 ch. [54]

R12: working in front loops only: *ch 1, sk 1, (flo dc 2 in each st, ch 3 picot st, flo dc 2 in each st), ch 1 , sk 1, flo ss 1*; after the first set, then rep * * 12 times, 1 ss, 1 ch, cut and leave a tail

SMALL FLOWER PETALS

Go to where you placed the stitch marker on the stamen and join the yarn
Working in front loops only
R9: *ch 8, from 2nd st from hook, sc 7, sk 1, ss 2*, after the first set, then repeat ** 17 times, 1 ss, 1 ch

EDGING OF PETALS

add iron wire; *blo sc 1, blo hdc 1 , blo dc 3, blo hdc 1, blo sc 1, in the same st (blo sc 1, ch 1 picot st, blo sc 1), blo hdc 1, blo dc 3, blo hdc 1, blo sc 1, sk 1, ss 1 * After the first set, then repeat **17 times, 1 ss,1 ch, cut and leave a tail
Hide the tail with a darning needle, Twist the wire tightly and hide

BIG FLOWER
PETALS

Go to where you placed the
stitch marker on R10 the
stamen and join the yarn
Working in front loops only
R10: *ch 10, from 2nd st
from hook, sc 9, sk 1, ss 2*
After the first set, then repeat
** 17 times, 1 ss,1 ch

EDGING OF
PETALS

add iron wire, * blo sc 1, blo
hdc 1, blo dc 5, blo hdc 1, blo
sc 1, in the same st (blo sc
1, ch 1 picot st, blo sc 1), blo
hdc 1, blo dc 5, blo hdc 1, blo
sc 1, sk 1, ss 1 * After the
first set, then rep ** 17
times.1 ss,1 ch, cut and
leave a tail
Hide the tail with a darning
needle, Twist the wire tightly
and hide

LEAF

Let's start with foundation
chain: ch 21
R1: add iron wire, in the 4th
st from hook, tr 2 in each
stitch, tr 8, dc 3, hdc 3, sc 2,

sc 3 in last st, (do not turn working on the other side); sc 2, hdc 3, dc 3, tr 8, tr 2 in each st, ch 3, ss on bottom of 1st ch.

R2: ch 3, in the same st (sc 1, hdc 1), in the same st (dc 1, tr 1); tr 8, dc 4, hdc 3, sc 2, sc 3 in last st, (do not turn, working on the other side); sc 2, hdc 3, dc 4, tr 8, in the same st (tr 1, dc 1), in the same st (hdc 1, sc 1); ch 3, ss at base of ch 3.

R3: ch 3, sc 2 in next st, hdc 2 in next st, dc 2 in next st, dc 9, hdc 5, sc 5, in the next st (sc 2, 2 ch picot st, sc 1); sc 5, hdc 5, dc 9, dc 2 in next st, hdc 2 in next st, sc 2 in next st, ch 3, ss at the base of 1st ch. Cut and leave a tail to join.

ASSEMBLE

Step 1: Bend one end of the stem and insert it into the middle of the flower sepals

Step 2: In the same steps, bend two flower stems and glue them on the sepals with hot melt adhesive

Step 3: Use the yarn of the same color as the sepals to sew with the stamen, leave an opening before the sewing ends, add fiberfill, and then sew the rest

Step 4: Use a green yarn and wrap the stem, add the leaf

Step 5: Continue wrap to the end, cut the tail and secure with hot melt adhesive

AGROSTEMMA
GITHAGO

Materials

- Yarn- light and dark pink, green, white, and brown
- Crochet hook-2.0mm
- Scissors
- Darning needle

- Stitch marker
- Flower rod – 30 cm long
- Iron wire- 0.5 mm and 0.7 mm
- Hot melt adhesive

PETALS

Make 5

Start with the foundation chain: 13 ch.

R1: Add wire, from the 2nd st of the hook, work 1 sc, 2 hdc, 2 dc, 2 htr, 3 tr, 2 tr in each st, and (2 tr, 1 dc, 1 ch, 1 ss, 1 ch, 1 dc, 2 tr). Work on another side, make(2 tr, 1 dc, 1 ch, 1 ss, 1 ch, 1 dc, 2 tr), followed by 2 tr in each st, 3 tr, 2 htr, 2 dc, 2 hdc, and 1 sc. 1 ss, cut and wrap the tail around the wire.

Take a dark pink yarn and take a strand of it. Sew on the petals to create the texture of the petals and make them more realistic.

SEPAL

Start with a magic ring.
R1-3: Work 5 sc in the round.
1 ss
R4: Make (6 ch, then work behind the vertical bar in the chain, and work 5 ss, 1 ss in the next st) Repeat 5 times. 1 ch, cut and weave the ends.

R5: Insert wire, then make 2 sc, sc2tog, 1 sc, sc2tog, 1 sc, and sc2tog. 1 ss and 1 ch
R6-7: Work 7 sc. 1 ss and 1 ch. add fiberfill
R8: Make 1 sc, sc2tog, 1 sc, sc2tog, and 1 sc. 1 ss.
R9: Make (6 ch, work behind the vertical bar in the chain, 5 ss, 1 ss in the next st) repeat 5 times. 1 ch, cut and weave the ends.

BUD WITHOUT FLOWER

R1: Start with a magic ring, 5 sc in the round. 1 ss and 1 ch
R2: Make (2 sc in each st) repeat 5 times. 1 ss and 1 ch
R3-4: Work 10 sc, 1 ss and 1 ch.

BUD WITH FLOWER

R1: Start with a magic ring, 5 sc in the round. 1 ss and 1 ch
R2: Make (2 sc in each st) repeat 5 times. 1 ss and 1 ch
R3-4: Work 10 sc, 1 ss and 1 ch.

R5: Insert wire, then make 2 sc, sc2tog, 1 sc, sc2tog, 1 sc, and sc2tog. 1 ss and 1 ch

R6-7: Work 7 sc. 1 ss and 1 ch. add fiberfill

R8: Make 1 sc, sc2tog, 1 sc, sc2tog, and 1 sc. 1 ss.

R9: Work front loop only (FLO): make (6 ch, then work behind the vertical bar in the chain, 5 ss, and 1 ss) repeat 5 times

R10: Change yarn, work back loops only (BLO): Make (5 ch, then work behind the vertical bar in the chain, 4 sc, 1 ss) repeat 5 times, 1 ss, 1 ch. Followed by (1 sc, 1 hdc, 1 dc, 3 dc in same st, 3 dc in same st, 1 dc, 1 hdc, 1 sc) repeat 5 times. cut and weave the ends.

LEAVES

Make 5
Start with the foundation chain: 15 ch, then work behind the 2nd st vertical bar in the chain, and 14 sc. cut and leave a tail.

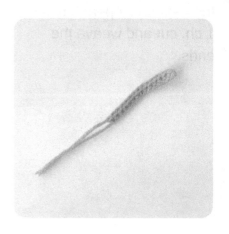

ASSEMBLE

Step 1: You'll need 4 short pieces of yarn and a wire. Fold the wire in half and tie the yarn to it. Use pliers to squeeze the wire tight. Then, take another piece of yarn and tie it with the existing yarn. Use a needle to loosen the yarns.

Weave the stem using green yarn and add the leaf. Keep weaving until it's done.

Step 2: Take the 5 crocheted Agrostemma Githago flower petals and arrange them one by one, and wrap pink yarn around the wire.

Step 3: Trim the stamens with scissors.
Step 4: Put the flower sepals of Agrostemma Githago under the flower petals.

Step 5: Now, take a flower rod and position the crocheted Agrostemma Githago flowers and buds. Use green yarn to weave them in place. Use hot melt adhesive to secure the end.

PRINCESS
SUKI ROSE

Materials

- Yarn – Dark and light pink, green
- Crochet hook – 2.0mm
- Scissors
- Darning needle

- Flower rod – 30 cm long
- Iron wire
- Hot melt adhesive
- Stitch marker

SMALL PETALS

Make 4
Start with a magic ring.
R1: work 2 ch, 6 hdc in the round. 1 ss in the first st. [6]
R2: work 3 ch, (2 dc in each st) after the first set, then repeat 5 times. 1 ss in the first st. [12]
R3: work 3 ch, (2 dc in each st) after the first set, then repeat 11 times. 1 ss in the first st, and 1 ch. [24]
Cut and leave a tail.

MIDDLE PETALS

Make 5
Start with a magic ring.
R1: work 2 ch, 8 hdc in the round. 1 ss in the first st.[8]
R2: work 3 ch, (2 dc in each st) after the first set, then repeat 7 times. 1 ss in the first st. [16]
R3: work 3 ch, (1 dc, 2 dc in each st) after the first set, then repeat 7 times. 1 ss in the first st, and 1 ch. [24] Cut and leave a tail.

BIG PETALS

Make 5
Start with a magic ring.
R1: work 2 ch, 12 hdc in the round. 1 ss in the first st. [12]

R2: work 3 ch, (2 dc in each st) after the first set, then repeat 11 times. 1 ss in the first st. [24]
R3: work 3 ch, (3 dc, 2 dc in each st) after the first set, then repeat 5 times. 1 ss in the first st, and 1 ch.[30]

LEAVES

Make 3
Let's start with the foundation chain: 12 ch
R1: Add wire, from 2nd st of hook, 1 sc, 1 hdc, 1 dc, 1 tr, 2 tr in each st, 1 tr, 2 tr in each st, 1 tr, 1 dc, 1 hdc; 3 sc in same st. 1 hdc, 1 dc, 1 tr, 2 tr in each st, 1 tr, 2 tr in each st, 1 tr, 1 dc, 1 hdc, 1 sc, 1 ss in the first st, and 1 ch. [22]

R2: (1 sc, 1 ch) after the first set, then repeat 12 times; (1 sc, 2 ch picot st, 1 sc), (1 sc, 1 ch) after the first set, then repeat 11 times, 1 sc, 1 ss in the first st. Leave the tail and wrap it around the wire

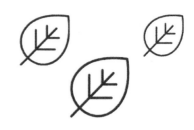

FLOWER SEPAL

Start with a magic ring.
R1: work 3 ch, 20 dc in the round. 1 ss in the first st.
R2: (10 ch, from 2nd st of hook, 2 ss, 2 sc, 2 hdc, 2 dc, 1 tr, sk 3, 1 ss in the next st) after the first set, then repeat 4 times. Finally, work 1 ch, cut and weave the end.

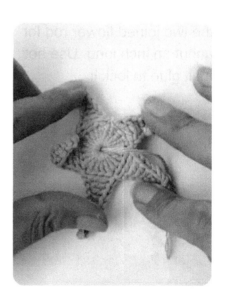

33

ASSEMBLE

1. Get your 3 leaves, combine them altogether by wrapping its stem with green yarn.

2. Wrap dark pink yarn on the two joined flower rod for about an inch long. Use hot melt glue to lock it

3. Get your one of the small petals and attached it to the flower rod where you wrap an inch dark pink yarn by wrapping it around.

4. After that, get your remaining 3 small petals and attached it to the first small petals that is attached on the flower rod. It must be overlapping with each other to achieve a rose outcome. You can follow the photos below.

5. Repeat the process on the 5 light pink middle petals. It must be overlapping to each other. Fasten it using hot melt glue so it will be attached to each other.

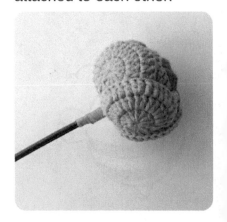

6. Follow it by putting the 5 light pink petals around the middle petals.

7. Wrap a green yarn below the flower for about an inch to hide the tail of the pink petals before inserting the sepal on the flower rod. Using hot melt glue, paste each part of the sepals on the flower.

8. Grab your green yarn and start wrapping it around the stem to hide the flower rod.

9. When you reached almost half of the flower rod, you can now add the 3 leaves on the stem.

10. Continue on wrapping the stem using green yarn up until you reach the end part of the flower rod.

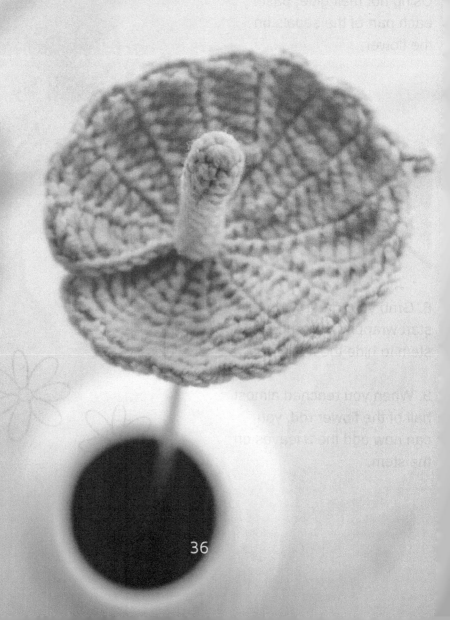

PINK
CHAMPION

Materials

- Yarn-yarn of three colors, pink, white, and green
- Flower rod – 16 inches long x 0.08 inches diameter (40cm x 2mm)
- Stitch marker
- Scissors
- Darning needle
- Hot melt adhesive
- Hook-2.5mm

FLOWER

Note: From R1-R14 is made using the Afghan Stitch technique.

Start with the foundation chain: Make 5 ch stitches and join with an ss in the first chain stitch to form a ring. 12 ch, Insert your hook behind the fifth stitches vertical bar in the chain below.

R1: 3 tr, 3 dc, and 2 sc.

R2: Make 4 ch, 3 tr, 3 dc, and 3 sc.

R3: Make 4 ch, work 2 tr in each stitch, 2 tr, 3 dc, and 3 sc.

R4: Make 4 ch, work 2 tr in each stitch, 3 tr, 3 dc, and 3 sc.

R5: Make 4 ch, work 2 tr in each stitch, 4 tr, 3 dc, and 3 sc.
R6: Make 4 ch, work 2 tr in each stitch, 1 tr, 2 dc, and 2 sc.
R7: Make 4 ch, work 2 trin each stitch, 3 tr, 5 dc, and 4 sc.
Make 5 ch, from the second stitch of the hook, and make 2 ss. Make 2 ch.

THE OTHER SIDE

R8: work 2 tr in each stitch, 5 tr, 4 dc, and 4 sc. (Close the last three loops in the return pass of the Afghan Stitch.)
R9: Make 4 ch, 5 tr, 5 dc, and 4 sc. (Close the last three loops in the return pass of the Afghan Stitch.)
R10: Make 4 ch, 3 tr, 2 dc, and 2 sc. (Close the last three loops in the return pass of the Afghan Stitch.)
R11: Make 4 ch, 6 tr, 3 dc, and 3 sc. (Close the last three loops in the return pass of the Afghan Stitch.)
R12: Make 4 ch, 5 tr, 3 dc, and 3 sc. (Close the last three loops in the return pass of the Afghan Stitch.)
R13: Make 4 ch, 4 tr, 3 dc, and 3 sc. (Close the last three loops in the return pass of the Afghan Stitch.)
R14: Make 4 ch, 3 tr, 3 dc, and 3 sc. (Close the last three loops in the return pass of the Afghan Stitch.)
R15: Switch to normal stitches (not Afghan stitches).

Make 5 ch, 3 tr, 2 dc, 1 hdc,
1 sc, 1 ss. cut and weave the
end.

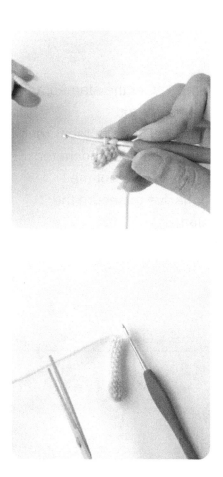

STAMEN

Using pink yarn, start with a
magic ring.
Rows 1-4: Work 6 sc in the
round.
Rows 5-12: Change to white
yarn and continue working 6
sc. 1 ss and cut the tail

ASSEMBLE

Step 1: Get the stamen and
the flower rod
Step 2: Then put the flower
rod inside your crocheted
stamen. Use hot melt
adhesive to secure the
stamen.

Step 1: Get the stamen and the flower rod

Step 2: Then put the flower rod inside your crocheted stamen. Use hot melt adhesive to secure the stamen.

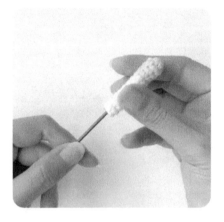

Step 4: Then use an existing yarn to wrap the flower rod to make it presentable.

Step 3: Get the flower then position it under the stamen. Use hot melt adhesive to secure the stamen at the center of the flower.

BIG THAI
ROSE

SMALL PETALS

Make 4
Start with a magic ring.
R1: work 5 sc in the round. 1
ss in the first st, and 1 ch.
R2: (2 sc in each st) * 5
times. 1 ss in the first st, and
1 ch.
R3: (1 sc, 2 sc in next st) * 5
times. 1 ss in the first st, and
1 ch.
R4: (1 sc, 2 sc in next st, 1
sc) * 5 times. 1 ss in the first
st, and 1 ch.
R5: (3 sc, 2 sc in next st) * 5
times. 1 ss in the first st, and
1 ch.
R6: (2 sc, 2 sc in next st, 2
sc) * 5 times. 1 ss in the first
st, and 1 ch.

R7: work 11 sc, 2 hdc in next st, 2 hdc, 2 hdc in next st, 2 hdc, 2 hdc in next st, 12 sc. 1 ss in the first st, and 1 ch.
R8: work 11 sc, (2 dc in next st) * 10 times, 12 sc. 1 ss in the first st.
R9: 3 ch, turn, 2 dc in next st, 1 dc, 1 ch. Cut off and leave a tail.

MIDDLE PETALS

Make 4
Start with a magic ring.
R1: work 5 sc in the round. 1 ss in the first st, and 1 ch.
R2: (2 sc in each st) * 5 times. 1 ss in the first st, and 1 ch.
R3: (1 sc, 2 sc in next st) * 5 times. 1 ss in the first st, and 1 ch.
R4: (1 sc, 2 sc in next st, 1 sc) * 5 times. 1 ss in the first st, and 1 ch.
R5: (3 sc, 2 sc in next st) * 5 times. 1 ss in the first st, and 1 ch.
R6: (2 sc, 2 sc in next st, 2 sc) * 5 times. 1 ss in the first st, and 1 ch.

R7: (5 sc, 2 sc in next st) * 5 times. 1 ss in the first st, and 1 ch.
R8: work 6 sc, (2 hdc in next st, then 6 hdc) * 3 times. 2 hdc in next st, 7 sc. 1 ss in the first st.
R9: work 3 ch, 7 dc, (2 dc in next st) * 12 times. (petal tip: 2 dc in next st, 2 ch picot st, 2 dc in next st); (2 dc in next st) * 12 times, then work 7 dc. 1 ss in the first st
R10: 3 ch, turn, 2 dc in next st, 1 dc, 1 ch. Cut off and leave a tail.

BIG PETALS

Make 5

Start with a magic ring.

R1: work 5 sc in the round. 1 ss in the first st, and 1 ch.

R2: (2 sc in next st) * 5 times. 1 ss in the first st, and 1 ch.

R3: (1 sc, 2 sc in next st) * 5 times. 1 ss in the first st, and 1 ch.

R4: (1 sc, 2 sc in next st, 1 sc) * 5 times. 1 ss in the first st, and 1 ch.

R5: (3 sc, 2 sc in next st) * 5 times. 1 ss in the first st, and 1 ch.

R6: (2 sc, 2 sc in next st, 2 sc) * 5 times. 1 ss in the first st, and 1 ch.

R7: (5 sc, 2 sc in next st) * 5 times. 1 ss in the first st, and 1 ch.

R8: (3 sc, 2 sc in next st, 3 sc) * 5 times. 1 ss in the first st.

R9: work 2 ch, 7 hdc, (2 hdc in next st, 3 hdc) * 6 times; 2 hdc in next st, 8 hdc. 1 ss in the first st.

R10: work 3 ch, 7 dc, (2 dc in next st) * 16 times. (petal tip: 2 dc in next st, 2 ch picot st, 2 dc in next st); (2 dc in next st) * 16 times; 7 dc. 1 ss in the first st.

R11: work 3 ch, turn, 2 dc in next st, 1 dc, 1 ch. Cut off and leave a tail.

44

FLOWER SEPAL

Start with a magic ring.

R1: work 5 sc in the round. 1 ss in the first st, and 1 ch.

R2: (2 sc in next st) * 5 times. 1 ss in the first st, and 1 ch.

R3: (1 sc, 2 sc in next st) * 5 times. 1 ss in the first st, and 1 ch.

R4: (1 sc, 2 sc in next st, 1 sc) * 5 times. 1 ss in the first st, and 1 ch.

R5-R7: make 20 sc in each round. 1 ss in the first st, and 1 ch.

R8: Note: After finishing one sepal, cut the yarn at the top and use a new yarn to make the next one, a total of five sepals.

Step 1: Work 4 sc, 1 ch, turn

Step 2: 2 sc in next st, 1 sc, 2 sc in next st, 1 sc, 1 ch, turn

Step 3: Work 6 sc, 1 ch, turn

Step 4: Work 6 sc, 1 ch, turn

Step 5: Sc2tog, 4 sc, 1 ch, turn

Step 6: Sc2tog, 3 sc, 1 ch, turn

Step 7: Sc2tog, 2 sc, 1 ch, turn

Step 8: Sc2tog, 1 sc, 1 ch, turn

Step 9: Sc2tog, 1 ch, turn

Step 10: 1 hdc, 1 ch. cut off and leave a tail.

BIG LEAF

Start with the foundation
chain: 15 ch
R1: add wire, 1 sc, 1 dc, 2 tr,
1 dtr, 2 dtr in next st, 1 dtr, 2
dtr in next st, 1 dtr, 2 tr, 1 dc,
1 hdc; (leaf tip: 3 sc in same
st); 1 hdc, 1 dc, 2 tr, 1dtr, 2
dtr in next st, 1 dtr, 2 dtr in
next st, 1 dtr, 2 tr, 1 dc, 1 sc.
1 ss in the first st , and 1 ch.
R2: (1 sc, 2 ch) * 16 times;
(in the same st: 1 sc, 2 ch
picot st, 1 sc); (2 ch, 1 sc)
*16 times. 1 ss in the first st.
cut off and wrap the tail
around the wire.

SMALL LEAVES

Make 2
Start with the foundation
chain: 12 ch
R1: add wire, 1 sc, 1 dc, 1 tr,
2 dtr, 2 dtr in next st, 1 dtr, 1
tr, 1 dc, 1 hdc; (leaf tip: 3 sc
in same st); 1 hdc, 1 dc, 1 tr,
1 dtr, 2 dtr in next st, 2 dtr, 1
tr, 1 dc, 1 sc, 1 ss in the first
st, and 1 ch.
R2: (1 sc, 2 ch) * 12 times,
(in the same st: 1 sc, 2 ch
picot st, 1 sc); (2 ch, 1 sc) *
12 times. 1 ss in the first st.
cut off and wrap the tail
around the wire.

ASSEMBLE

Assemble the Leaves: Get the small and big leaves, tie them together and tilt both two small leaves sideways.

Assemble Big Thai Rose

Step 1: Take 3 flower rods, and wrap the top with yellow yarn. Use hot melt adhesive to keep the end of the yarn in place.
Step 2: Have all the petals ready: small, medium, and large. Glue them one after another onto the rod. Find the yarn near the flower's base (sepal) and tie it. Then, use hot melt adhesive so it stays tied.

Step 3: Take the flower base (sepal). Slide the rod into its center. Glue it so it stays attached to the flower.

ASSEMBLE

Step 4: Wrap the rod in green yarn for the stem. Add leaves as you wrap. When done, use hot melt adhesive on the end to keep everything tight.

NARCISSUS

SMALL PETALS

Make 3
Start with the foundation chain: 13 ch
R1: From the 2nd st of the hook, make 1 sc, 1 hdc, followed by (1 dc, 2 dc in each st) repeat 3 times, 2 dc, 1 hdc, 3 sc in same st, 1 hdc, 2 dc, (2 dc in each st, 1 dc) repeat 3 times, 1 hdc, and 1 sc. 1 ss and 1 ch
R2: Add wire, then work 2 sc, 9 hdc, 4 sc, 3 sc in the same st, 4 sc, 9 hdc, 1 sc, and 2 sc in each st. 1 ss, cut and wrap the tail around the wire.

BIG PETALS

Make 3
Start with the foundation chain: 13 ch
R1: From the 2nd st of the hook, make 2 sc, 1 hdc, followed by (2 dc in each st, 1 dc) repeat 3 times, 2 hdc, 3 sc in the same st, 2 hdc, (1 dc, 2 dc in each st) repeat 3 times, 2 hdc, and 1 sc. 1 ss and 1 ch
R2: Add wire, then work 3 sc, 6 hdc, 6 sc, 3 sc in the same st, 6 sc, 6 hdc, 2 sc, and 2 sc in each st. 1 ss, cut and wrap the tail around the wire.

COROLLA

R1: Start with a magic ring then work 10 sc in the round. 1 ss, 1 ch
R2: Make (1 sc, 2 sc in each st) repeat 5 times. 1 ss, 1 ch
R3: Make (4 sc, 2 sc in each st) repeat 3 times. 1 ss, 1 ch
R4-6: Work 18 sc in each round. 1 ss, 1 ch
R7: Make (5 sc, 2 sc in each st) repeat 3 times. 1 ss, 1 ch
R8-10: Work 21 sc in each round. 1 ss, 1 ch
R11: Make (6 sc, 2 sc in each st) repeat 3 times. 1 ss
R12: (in the same st: work 2 ch, 1 ss) repeat 24 times. Cut and weave the ends.

STAMENS

Make 7
Using yellow yarn, take out 3 strands, then wrap it in the middle of the wire, fold it in half, and continue wrapping to the end.

SMALL LEAF

Start with the foundation chain: 45 ch
R1: From the 2nd st of the hook, make 5 sc, 30 hdc, 8 sc, 3 sc in the same st, 8 sc, 30 hdc, and 5 sc. 1 ss, 1 ch.
R2: Add wire, then work 44 sc, 3 sc in the same st, and 44 sc. 1 ss, cut and weave the ends.

BIG LEAF

Start with the foundation chain: 55 ch
R1: From the 2nd st of the hook, work 5 sc, 40 hdc, 8 sc, 3 sc in the same st, 8 sc, 40 hdc, and 5 sc.
R2: Add wire, then work 54 sc, 3 sc in the same st, and 54 sc. 1 ss, cut and weave the ends.

ASSEMBLE

Step 1: Tie the stamens together tightly using green yarn, and then use hot glue to make sure it stays in place.

Step 2: Take the Corolla (center) of the crocheted Narcissus and place the stamens in the middle.

Step 3: Arrange the small petals one after another, then alternate big petals. Use hot glue to stick them together. Then, tie them together with green yarn and secure the end with hot melt glue.

Step 4: Attach the flower rod to the end of the wrapped wire. Continue wrapping the stem, and as you do, carefully attach the leaves. Finally, use hot melt glue to secure the end of the crocheted Narcissus flower.

DANDELION

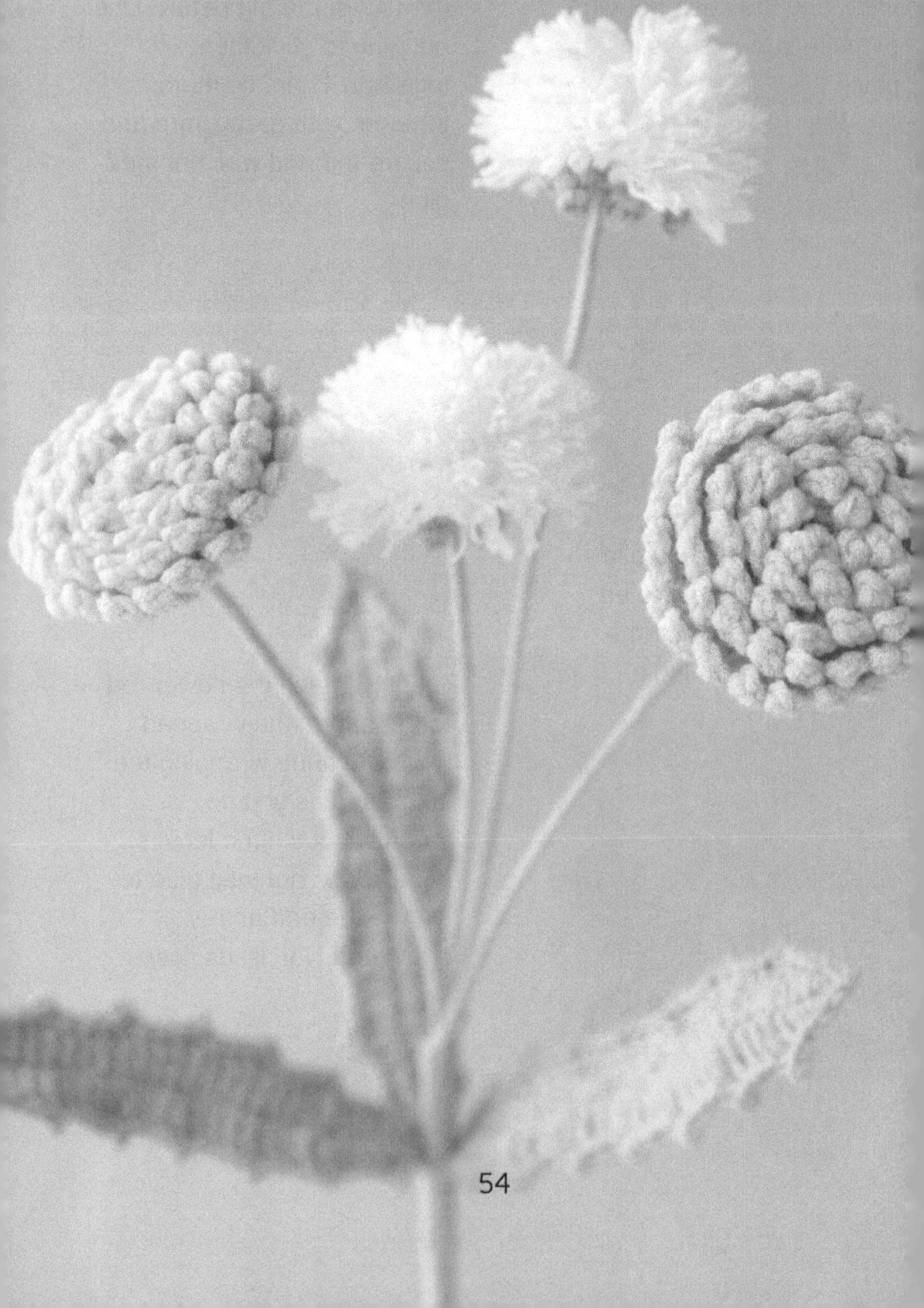

Materials

- Yarn- yellow, white, and green
- Crochet hook-2.0mm
- Scissors
- Darning needle
- Stitch marker

- Fiberfill
- Flower rod – 30 cm long
- Iron wire- 0.5 mm and 0.7 mm
- Hot melt adhesive

FLOWER BASE HOLDERS

(Note: all work back loops only)

R1: Start with a magic ring, 4 sc in the round. 1 ss, 1 ch

R2: (2 sc in each st) Repeat 4 times . 1 ss, 1 ch

R3: (2 sc in each st) Repeat 2 times, 1 sc, (2 sc in each st) Repeat 2 times, 1 sc, (2 sc in each st) Repeat 2 times. 1 ss, 1 ch

R4: (2 sc in each st, 1 sc, 2 sc in each st, 1 sc, 2 sc in each st, 2 sc) repeat 2 times. 1 ss, 1 ch

R5: (2 sc in each st, 4 sc) repeat 4 times. 1 ss, 1 ch. cut and weave the ends.

PETALS

(Note: all work front loops only)

R1: use yellow yarn, (work 4 ch, from 2nd st of hook, 3 ss. 1 ss in the first st. Then 4 ch in the same st, from 2nd st of hook, 3 ss, 1 ss in the next st) Repeat 4 times.

R2: (work 5 ch, from 2nd st of hook, 4 ss, 1 ss in the next st) Repeat 8 times

R3: (work 5 ch, from 2nd st of hook, 4 ss, 1 ss in the next st) Repeat 11 times

R4: (work 5 ch, from 2nd st of hook, 4 ss, 1 ss in the next st) Repeat 17 times

R5: (work 5 ch, from 2nd st of hook, 4 ss, 1 ss in the next st) Repeat 21 times. 1 ch, cut off and weave the ends.

SEPALS

Make 2

R1: start with 4 sc in the round. 1 ss, 1 ch.

R2: work 4 sc, 1 ss, 1 ch.

R3: (2 sc in each st) repeat 4 times, 1 ss, 1 ch.

R4: (1 sc, 2 sc in each st) repeat 4 times, 1 ss, 1 ch.

R5: (2 sc, 2 sc in each st) repeat 4 times, 1 ss, 1 ch.

R6: work 16 sc, 1 ss, 1 ch.

R7: (1 sc, 1 ch picot st, 1 ss) repeat 16 times, 1 ss, 1 ch. cut and weave the ends.

ASSEMBLING

1. Take a 0.7mm iron wire and fold it in half; insert it into the middle of the sepal, then fix the dandelion flower and the sepal with hot melt glue, and lastly, stuff it with fiberfill before closing it.

2. Wrap the iron wire with green yarn and fix the tail with hot melt glue

WHITE FLOWERS

Make 2

Step 1: Wrap the white yarn around your fingers, use a piece of iron wire to pass through the middle, fold it in half, and tighten it.

Step 2: Cut from the middle of the yarn and use a needle to loosen the yarn

SEPALS FOR WHITE FLOWER

Make 2

R1: Start with 5 sc in the round then 1 ss.

R2: (5 ch, then from 2nd st of the hook, make 1 ss, 1 sc, 2 hdc, and 1 ss) repeat 5 times. 1 ch, cut, and weave the ends.

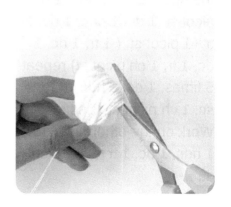

Step 3: Insert in the middle of the sepal, fix with hot melt glue, and trim white flowers.
Step 4: Wrap the iron wire with green yarn and fix the tail with hot melt glue.

(1 dc, 1 dc, 1 tr, 1 tr+1 ch picot st) repeat 5 times. 1 dc, 1 hdc, 1 dc, 1 dc+1 ch picot st, 1 hdc, 1 sc. 1 ss, cut and weave the ends.

LEAVES

Make 3
R1: Start with the foundation chain: 32 ch,
R2: Add wire, from 2nd st of the hook, 1 sc, 1 hdc, 1 dc+1 picot st, 1 dc, 1 hdc, 1 dc, 1 tr +1 picot st, (1 tr, 1 dc, 1 dc, 1 tr, 1 ch picot st) repeat 5 times, 1 dc, 1 hdc, 1 sc. 2 sc, 1 ch picot st, 1 sc.
Work on the other side: 1 sc, 1 hdc, 1 dc, 1 tr+ 1 ch picot st,

ASSEMBLE

Step 1: Arrange dandelions and white flowers alternately and wrap them with green yarn.
Step 2: Then wrap it around the stem, add 3 leaves, wrap it to the end, and fix it with hot melt glue.

AISHA ROSE

Materials

- Yarn- purple and green
- Crochet hook-2.0mm
- Scissors
- Darning needle
- Stitch marker

- Iron wire- 0.5 mm
- Hot melt adhesive
- Flower rod – 30 cm long

SMALL PETALS

Start with a magic ring.
R1: Make 5 sc in the round.
1 ss, 1 ch
R2: Make (2 sc in each st)
Repeat 5 times. 1 ss, 1 ch
R3: Make (1 sc, 2 sc in each st) Repeat 5 times. 1 ss, 1 ch
R4: Make (2 sc, 2 sc in each st) Repeat 5 times. 1 ss, 1 ch
R5: Make (3 sc, 2 sc in each st) Repeat 5 times. 1 ss, 1 ch
R6: Make (4 sc, 2 sc in each st) Repeat 5 times. 1 ss, 1 ch
R7: Work 11 sc, followed by 2 hdc in each st, 2 hdc, 2 hdc in each st, 2 hdc, 2 hdc in each st, and 12 sc. 1 ss, 1 ch
R8: Work 11 sc, followed by (2 dc in each st) Repeat 10 times, and 12 sc. 1 ss, 1 ch. cut and leave a tail.

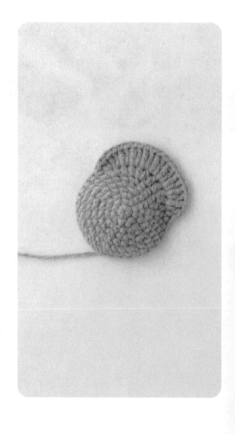

60

BIG PETALS

Make 5
Start with a magic ring.
R1: Make 5 sc in the round.
1 ss, 1 ch
R2: Make (2 sc in each st)
Repeat 5 times. 1 ss, 1 ch
R3: Make (1 sc, 2 sc in each
st) Repeat 5 times. 1 ss, 1 ch
R4: Make (2 sc, 2 sc in each
st) Repeat 5 times. 1 ss, 1 ch
R5: Make (3 sc, 2 sc in each
st) Repeat 5 times. 1 ss, 1 ch
R6: Make (4 sc, 2 sc in each
st) Repeat 5 times. 1 ss, 1 ch
R7: Make (5 sc, 2 sc in each
st) Repeat 5 times. 1 ss, 1 ch
R8: Work 6 sc, followed by 2
hdc in each st, 6 hdc, 2 hdc
in each st, 6 hdc, 2 hdc in
each st, 6 hdc, 2 hdc in each
st, and 7 sc. 1 ss.
R9: 3 ch, Work 7 dc, followed
by (3 dc in same st) repeat
25 times, and 7 dc. 1 ss, 1
ch. cut and leave a tail.

FLOWER SEPALS

Start with a magic ring.
R1: work 5 sc in the round. 1
ss, 1 ch
R2: (2 sc in each st) Repeat
5 times. 1 ss, 1 ch
R3: Work 10 sc. 1 ss, 1 ch
R4: (1 sc, 2 sc in each st)
repeat 5 times. 1 ss, 1 ch
R5: (2 sc, 2 sc in each st)
repeat 5 times. 1 ss, 1 ch
R6: (3 sc, 2 sc in each st)
Repeat 5 times. 1 ss
R7: (work 13 ch, then from
the 2nd st of the hook, make
3 sc, 2 hdc, 2 dc, 2 tr, 3 dtr,
sk 4, and 1 ss) Repeat 5
times. 1 ss, 1 ch. cut and
weave the ends.

LEAF

Start with the foundation chain: 13 ch

R1: From the 2nd st of the hook, add wire, then make 1 sc, 1 hdc, 2 dc, 4 tr, 2 dc, 1 hdc, 3 sc in the same st, 1 hdc, 2 dc, 4 tr, 2 dc, 1 hdc, and 1 sc. 1 ss, 1 ch

R2: Make (1 sc, 2 ch picot st, 1 sc, 2 ch), 1 sc, 2 ch, then repeat, and end with 1 sc. 1 ss. cut and wrap it around the wire.

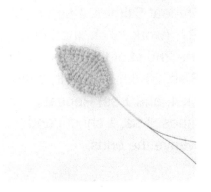

ASSEMBLE

Step 1: Leaf Arrangement of Aisha Rose

Gather the 3 crocheted aisha rose leaves.

Attach the 3 leaves together, aligning their bases.

Securely sew them together using green yarn.

Use hot melt adhesive to secure the ends of the yarn and leaves in place.

Position the two rose leaves side by side, forming a tilted arrangement.

Set aside the assembled leaves.

Step 2: Assembling the Petals of Aisha Rose

Take 2 flower rods and attach them together using green yarn.

Secure the joint with hot melt adhesive for added stability.

Arrange all the petals of crocheted Aisha Rose side by side.

Secure each petal in place using hot melt adhesive.

Use the green yarn to neatly sew over any existing yarn for a clean finish.

Continue to weave the flower rod with the green yarn. While weaving attach the leaves of Aisha Rose alongside the flower rod. Use hot melt adhesive to firmly secure the end.

3: Attaching the Flower Sepal, the Flower, and the Leaves of Aisha Rose
Position the flower sepals beneath the assembled crocheted flower of Aisha Rose. Secure the sepals in place using hot melt adhesive.

Materials

- Yarn – white, yellow, green (You can change the color according to your needs)
- Crochet hook-2.0mm
- Scissors

- Stitch marker
- Flower rod
- Iron wire
- Hot melt adhesive
- Darning needle

PETALS

Make 8

R1: Start with the foundation chain: 7 ch

R2: from 2nd st of hook, 2 sc, 1 hdc, 2 dc, 7 dc in the same st, then 2 dc, 1 hdc, 2 sc, 1 ss in the first stitch.

R3: make 4 ch, add wire, from 2nd st of hook, 3 sc; (1 sc, 1 ch) * 7 times, (in the same st: 1 sc, 2 ch, 1 sc) * 3 times, (1 ch, 1 sc) * 7 times, 3 sc, 1 ss in the first stitch of the row.

Cut extra yarn and wrap the wire with the tail.

STAMENS

Start with a magic ring.
R1: Work 6 sc in the round. 1 ss in the first stitch, 1 ch. [6]
R2: (2 sc in each st) * 6 times, 1 ss in the first stitch of the row, 1 ch. [12]
R3: work 12 sc, 1 ss, 1 ch. [12]
R4: (sc2tog) * 6 times. [6]
Take a flower rod, bend one end and stuff it into the stamen. cut the yarn and leave a tail. use the needle to weave in extra yarn and seal the bottom.

R1: add wire, from 2nd st of hook, 24 sc, 3 sc in the same st, then work 24 sc. 1 ss in the first stitch.
Cut extra yarn, Wrap the wire with yarn, then cut. Secure the yarn with hot melt glue.

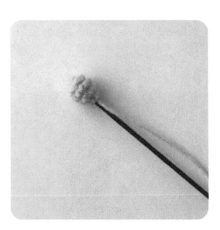

LEAF

Start with the foundation chain: 25 ch

ASSEMBLE

Step 1: Surround the eight petals in turn with the stamen. Wrap the petals and stem tightly with green yarn.

Step 2: Add the leaf and continue wrapping to the end of the stem. Secure the end with hot melt adhesive, then cut the yarn.

DAHLIA

Materials

- Yarn-four colors,(light and dark blue, cream, green)
- Hook- 2.5mm
- Flower rod – 16 inches long x 0.08 inches diameter (40cm x 2mm)

- Iron wire – 0.02 inches diameter (0.5mm)
- Darning Needle
- Stitch Marker
- Scissors
- Fiberfill
- Hot Melt Adhesive

PETALS

Start with a magic ring.
R1: ch 2, work 2 unfinished dc puffs 7 times, then ss in the second stitch to join.

After the first set, repeat 5 times.

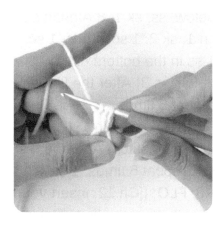

R2: FLO: {(ch 5, insert your hook behind the first stitch's vertical bar in the chain below; then make 1 ss, 1 sc, 1 hdc, 1 sc, 1 ss), ss}.

R3: BLO: ss 1, ch 1, (sc 2 in each stitch) After the first set, repeat 5 times. 1 ss

R4: FLO: {[Ch 7, insert your hook behind the first stitch's vertical bar in the chain below, 1 ss, work 6 Afghan sc, sk 1, 4 sc, 1 ss in the bottom of the petal], ss 2} After the first set, repeat 5 times.

R5: Change yarn color, BLO: ss 1, 1 ch, (sc, sc 2 in each stitch) After the first set, repeat 5 times. 1 ss

R6: FLO: {[Ch 10, insert your hook behind the first stitch's vertical bar in the chain below, ss, sk 1, 8 Afghan sc, ch 1, sk 2, 1 sc, 4 hdc, 1 sc, 1 ss in the bottom of the petal], ss 3} After the first set, repeat 5 times.

R7: BLO: ss 1, ch 1, (2 sc, sc 2 in each stitch) After the first set, repeat 5 times. 1 ss

R8: FLO: {[Ch 12, insert your hook behind the first stitch's vertical bar in the chain below, ss, sk 1, (use Afghan stitch, 1 sc, sk 1, 6 dc, 2 sc), ch 1, sk 2, 1 sc, 5 hdc, 1 sc,

ss in the bottom], ss 3} After the first set, repeat 7 times.
R9: BLO: ss 1, ch 1, (3 sc, sc 2 in each stitch) After the first set, repeat 5 times. 1 ss
R10: FLO: {[Ch 14, insert your hook behind the first stitch's vertical bar in the chain below, ss, sk 1, (use Afghan stitch,1 sc, sk 1, 8 dc, 2 sc), ch 1, sk 2,1 sc,1 hdc, 4 dc, ch 1, 1 dc, 1 hdc, 1 sc, ss in the bottom], ss 3} After the first set, repeat 9 times.

R11: Change yarn color, BLO: ss 1, ch 1, (4 sc, sc 2 in each stitch) * 6 times. 1 ss

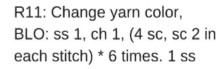

R12: FLO: {[Ch 16, insert your hook behind the first stitch's vertical bar in the chain below, ss, sk 1, (use Afghan stitch, 1 sc, sk 1, 10 dc, 2 sc), ch 1, sk 2, 1 sc, 1 hdc, 5 dc, ch 1, 2 dc, 1 hdc, 1 sc, ss in the bottom], ss 3}

After the first set, repeat 11 times.

R13: BLO: ss 1, ch 1, and 36 sc. 1 ss

R14: work front loops only: FLO{[18 ch, Insert your hook behind the first stitches vertical bar in the chain below: 1 ss, sk 1,(Use Afghan stitch, 1 sc, sk 1, 12 dc, 2 sc), 1 ch, sk 2, 1 sc, 1 hdc, 5 dc, 1 ch, 4 dc, 1 hdc, 1 sc, 1 ss in the bottom], 3 ss} After the first set, repeat 11 times.

72

R15: Change yarn color to green, and BLO: (1 sc, sc2 together) * 12 times, 1 ss, 1 ch

ss 2} After the first set, repeat 7 times.

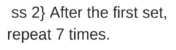

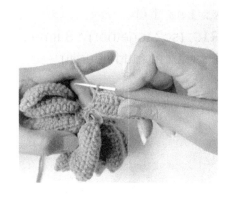

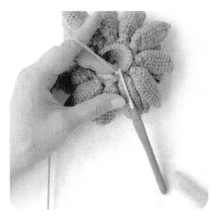

R16: (1 sc, sc2 together) * 8 times, 1 ss.
R17: FLO: {[Ch 8, insert your hook behind the first stitch's vertical bar in the chain below, 1 ss, work 7 Afghan single crochets, turn, sk 1, 5 sc],

R18: BLO: ss 1, ch 1, and 16 sc. 1 ss, 1 ch.
R19: (sc2 together) * 8 times. 1 ss, 1 ch. (add fiberfill)

R20: (sc2 together) * 4 times. 1 ss, cut and leave a tail.

LEAF

Make 2

Step 1: Start with a foundation ch 18.
Step 2: Add a wire, and ch 2.
Step 3: Insert your hook behind the second stitch's vertical bar in the chain below, 1 ss, 1 sc, 5 hdc, and 4 sc.
Step 4: Turn, insert your hook behind the second stitch's vertical bar in the chain below, 5 sc and 2 ss.
Step 5: Turn, ch 1, insert your hook behind the second stitch's vertical bar in the chain below, 1 ss, 1 sc, 2 hdc in each stitch, 3 hdc, 3 sc.

Step 6: Turn, insert your hook behind the second stitch's vertical bar in the chain below, 5 sc and 2 ss.
Step 7: Turn, chain 1, insert your hook behind the second stitch's vertical bar in the chain below, 1 ss, 1 sc, 2 hdc in each stitch, 5 hdc, 3 sc
Step 8: Turn, insert your hook behind the second stitch's vertical bar in the chain below, 5 sc and 2 ss.
Step 9: Turn, ch 1, insert your hook behind the second stitch's vertical bar in the chain below, 1 ss, 1 sc, 2 hdc in each stitch, 6 hdc, 1 sc, 1 ss, ch 1, 15 sc, 2 ss.

OTHER SIDE OF THE LEAF

Step 10: Turn, chain 1, insert your hook behind the second stitch's vertical bar in the chain below, 1 ss, 1 sc, 2 hdc in each stitch, 5 hdc, 3 sc.
Step 11: Turn, insert your hook behind the second

stitch's vertical bar in the chain below, 5 sc and 2 ss.
Step 12: Turn, chain 1, insert your hook behind the second stitch's vertical bar in the chain below, 1 ss, 1 sc, 2 hdc in each stitch, 5 hdc, 3 sc.
Step 13: Turn, insert your hook behind the second stitch's vertical bar in the chain below, 5 sc and 2 ss.
Step 14: Turn, ch 1, insert your hook behind the second stitch's vertical bar in the chain below, 1 ss, 1 sc, 2 hdc in each stitch, 5 hdc, 1 sc, 2 ss. cut and leave a tail

SMALL LEAF

Make 2
Step 1: Start with a foundation ch 14.
Step 2: Add a wire, and ch 2.
Step 3: Insert your hook behind the second stitch's vertical bar in the chain below, 1 ss, 1 sc, 4 hdc, and 4 sc.
Step 4: Turn, insert your hook behind the second stitch's vertical bar in the chain below, 4 sc and 2 ss.

Step 5: Turn, ch 1, insert your hook behind the second stitch's vertical bar in the chain below, 1 ss, 1 sc, 2 hdc in each stitch, 4 hdc, 3 sc.
Step 6: Turn, insert your hook behind the second stitch's vertical bar in the chain below, 4 sc and 2 ss.
Step 7: Turn, ch 1, insert your hook behind the second stitch's vertical bar in the chain below, 1 ss, 1 sc, 1 hdc, 2 hdc in each stitch, 3 hdc, 1 hdc, 1 sc. (in the same stitch, 1 ss, ch 1, sc 1), 10 sc, 2 ss.
Step 8: Turn, ch 1, insert your hook behind the second stitch's vertical bar in the chain below, 1 ss, sc, 2 hdc in each stitch, 4 hdc, 3 sc.

Step 9: Turn, insert your hook behind the second stitch's vertical bar in the chain below, 4 sc and 2 ss.
Step 10: Turn, ch 1, insert your hook behind the second stitch's vertical bar in the chain below, 1 ss, 1 sc, 1 hdc, 2 hdc in each stitch, 3 hdc, 1 sc, 2 ss. cut and leave a tail

ASSEMBLE LEAVES

Step 1: Wrap the tail of the leaves around the wire, and secure it with hot melt adhesive.
Step 2: Wrap one large leaf and two small leaves together， and secure with hot melt adhesive.

ASSEMBLE THE DAHLIA FLOWER AND LEAVES

Step 3: Get the flower rod then attach it to the center of the flower.
Step 4: Wrap the rod with the yarn, and while wrapping at attached the leaves to its designated area.
Step 5: Secure the end of flower rod the with hot melt adhesive.
Step 6: Secure the sepals to the petals with hot melt adhesive.

Thank you

67460401R00046

CROCHET
Flower Garden

CREATIVE PATTERNS FOR FLORAL MASTERPIECES

Step into a world of vibrant colors and delicate petals with 'Crochet Flower Garden.' This enchanting book is your passport to crafting stunning floral masterpieces. Whether you're a seasoned crocheter or just starting your floral journey, this comprehensive guide will inspire and guide you through creating a breathtaking array of crochet flowers. From classic Roses and Sunflower to exotic Dahlia and Narcissus, you'll find a treasure trove of patterns to suit every skill level. Learn to crochet realistic blooms, whimsical buds, and intricate leaves that will transform your projects into works of art. Discover the joy of adding a touch of nature to your home decor, fashion accessories, or gifts with these delightful crochet flower patterns. Let your imagination blossom as you experiment with different colors, sizes, and combinations to create unique and personalized floral creations. With clear instructions, step-by-step photos, and helpful tips, this book is your go-to resource for crocheting beautiful flowers that will bring joy and beauty to your life.

ISBN 9798333771612

Blend Phonics
Lessons and
Stories

Donald L. Potter